About Student Government Solutions:

Student Government Solutions is focused on giving college and university student leaders all across the campus the resources and training they need to be successful. Our unique and innovative approach to planning and implementing projects helps students achieve their goals. The objective is to help build outstanding student leaders through providing high quality training materials, workshops and instruction, as well as project/issue specific aid for student leaders all across the country.

About the Author:

Eric Williams, author of the Essential Student Government Guide — College Edition and the High School & Middle School Edition, attended the University of California, Irvine where he studied Political Science, Economics and Management. In college Eric served as the Vice President of Administrative Affairs in the Associated Students of UC Irvine. During his time in student government Eric helped establish UC Irvine's first free legal clinic and a mentorship program aimed at boosting commuter student involvement on campus. He also served as a leader in the California Public Interest Group where he organized many media events and student mobilization campaigns. Eric was also involved in many clubs during his time in high school and college.

Written by Eric Williams

Acknowledgements and Legal Information

Table of Contents

Introduction

You're new to a club but you want to get more involved. You have some great plans and just need a few more skills to get them going. Maybe you've been in your group for a while and you're looking for something to breathe new life into the organization. You've been hung up on one issue or event for months, you want to get things off the ground and you're looking to this book for a little inspiration. *The Essential Student Clubs & Organizations Guide* is just what you need to make your organization a success and allow you to achieve all the goals you joined your organization for. This manual doesn't have a solution to every problem, but use the skills you learn here with your own creativity and you'll be able to build a great organization.

Clubs and organizations have always been a great place for students to gain valuable experience as a leader and a member of a group trying to accomplish a goal. You have a responsibility to the other members of your group to be a leader and help them have a great time. All clubs are different, but many need the same basic skills to be successful, like the ability to recruit new members, effectively plan events, and build future leaders. This guide will cover all the basic skills you'll need to build the organization and achieve the goals of your club.

Use this guide as a resource for setting and accomplishing your goals. The best way to start is to review each part of this guide and then focus in on what you specifically need. There are many fictional examples to help you understand the major concepts. Many of the strategies and tools in this manual you have never considered using before, but can be very beneficial. These new and exciting ideas will help launch your club into success. It's important to know what skills are available in this book so that you can learn how to use those tools as you need them. The more you know the more you'll be able to achieve in your organization, whether it is putting on the most amazing event your school has ever seen or raising funds for an important charity.

Chapter 1: Your Role in the Club

Even as a member of your club you have a great opportunity to make valuable contributions to not only your group but to your school as well. In order to accomplish your goals you need to think about where to start, what you want to work on and what your role means to you. Knowing your priorities helps you identify what you need to learn and what you have the opportunity to accomplish.

What Kind Leader Do You Want To Be?

Do you enjoy being in charge of what is going on? Were you always chosen to be a leader of groups you were involved in? Do you want to try to have a positive impact on your campus? Are you disappointed with how things have been run in the past and want to fix it for the better?

Despite sharing the common interest of the club, everyone brings a different set of priorities and interest to the organization. What do you want to accomplish during your time in your organization? The key is to understand your strengths and objectives so that you can set a plan in motion to get it done. You need to have a personal sense of direction in place so that you will be able to achieve your goals by using the tools in this manual.

Helpful Questions to ask yourself:

1. What do I care about and why?
2. What are the top 3 issues that I feel are facing fellow students?
3. What are the issues facing my organization?
4. What are my unique skills?
5. How can my unique skills benefit my fellow club members?

Why Does Your Organization Exist?

Clubs exist for a variety of reasons. Some share a love of an activity like bicycling, other feel passionately about a particular political issue, while more just share an interest in a particular subject or career. Whatever the reason, it should be pretty obvious what your club is about, because that's the reason you joined it. However, at a very basic level your club has a function or a goal that it was created to achieve. This is some tangible result. The level at which this is being accomplished can be measured by the degree of investment and excitement from your organization's members. You should take the time to learn as much as possible about why the club was created and what it is supposed to provide.

Usually a club will have a constitution and other documents that state the mission of the organization and how it is supposed to be organized. When students at your campus first created your club they had a specific purpose in mind for the organization. This reason can be anything from creating a social environment for people with a common interest to a results oriented advocacy organization. The options are endless, but you need to understand what you're organization is about. You can use this understanding as a roadmap to steer you through your time as a student leader in your organization.

Your Role as Part of the Team
Club Leaders:

The official responsibilities vary between positions and from club to club, but one definition encompasses all of them. You were elected to represent your fellow club members and facilitate accomplishing the goals of the organization. This could mean you have a group of club members working on putting together a great event for the club, working with other clubs to make sure that all of your club members are represented, or just running the weekly club meeting.

This position requires you to be a leader, a planner and a motivator more than anything else. You are the official representative of the members of the organization and the face of the club on campus. It becomes your duty to seek out and identify problems within the organization and make sure that everything is running smoothly. It is your job to make sure everything gets done for the club, but not necessarily to do everything yourself.

Organizers/Coordinators:

You have volunteered to take on a leadership role in your organization by helping to achieve the goals of the club. You may be responsible for planning and organizing a major event, coordinating a social activity for the club, or going to meetings around campus on your club's behalf. These projects rely on your energy and enthusiasm to make it work and get it done. You can inspire the other club members to take action and accomplish the goals because you understand the details of the position. You have a great deal of responsibility serving in this role because the elected leaders who you work with don't have time to work on the details of your assignment and are relying on you to accomplish it instead.

Use this time as a training ground to use your own experience to test new ideas about leadership and strategies for success in a relatively low stress and low consequence environment. Try something out of the box and don't let the fear of failure keep you from achieving your goals and learning something new about yourself.

Club Members and Volunteers:

Members and volunteers in an organization make up the majority of the club and help doing anything and everything that needs to get done to make the club successful. You have the opportunity to learn about many different aspects of the club and the common interest that binds everyone together. You can contribute your ideas and energy into ongoing projects and events. You can even start your own project. Volunteers are given real responsibilities and are often relied upon to help direct the logistics of an event or make sure that everyone is going to be in attendance at an important meeting. These duties take some of the load off of the elected leaders and organizers with busy schedules. Club members are in a great position to learn, grow, and become the next leaders in the organization.

Strengths of Clubs and Organizations

Invested Volunteers – Students in clubs are involved because of their own passion and interest in the topic of the club. This energy can generate many amazing leaders who genuinely care about the success of the club. When the odds are stacked against getting everything done, the enthusiasm your club members have for the organization can make everything happen.

Structure – The structure that exists for the organization has usually evolved over many years to help the club run smoothly in a way that is specific to that organization and the problems that typically come up. That doesn't mean it can't be improved upon, but you don't have to start from scratch every time new leaders take charge of the organization.

Faculty Advisor – Many clubs have a dedicated advisor either as part of the student services division of the school administration or an advisor from the teaching faculty which has some connection to the subject of interest. These people can have many years of experience both in the topic of the club and just common problems that club leaders and members might face trying to put on programs. These people can be invaluable in giving you advice about how to get stuff done.

History – Clubs have built up relationships with other clubs as brother/sister organization like fraternities/sororities, communal organization with similar topics like a group of service clubs or even a school council of all of the club leaders. They also have history with many administrators and faculty on campus with similar interests as the club. You can foster these relationships by continuing to keep in contact and asking for help when you need it.

Summary

Throughout this section we mainly focused on identifying and understanding your role in your organization. With your new roles and responsibilities it is important to figure out what you want to accomplish and what drives you as a leader and a member of your club. The more you're able to understand about yourself and about the group you belong to, the more you'll be able to accomplish your goals and those of the organization. Keep in mind the unique opportunities your club provides and what it will allow you to do.

Chapter 2: Club Organization

The major roles in your organization are to serve as a team member, a leader and a decision maker for the club. In any position you'll be asked to make decisions for the group and take part in a major aspect of the club. Decision making is not easy for most people to do, and sometimes you'll get it wrong. The tools in this chapter will help make that job easier by identifying many of the problematic areas and giving you tips to resolve them.

Structure & Organization

The leadership positions in your club should reflect the priorities of the group and the needs that certain activities entail. Each of these roles have the capacity to contribute to the club and each have their own unique challenges. Roles are flexible and can change the structure and purpose of your group.

- **President**—The role of president in a club is to coordinate all the other leaders within the group and to make sure everything is getting done. Typically the president will run the club meetings and facilitate the flow of information from the other leaders to the club members. They serve as the face of the organization and work with other club leaders and school administrators. Don't do all the work: delegate and coordinate.

- **Vice President**—The role of the vice president can vary from club to club, but their role should be the most flexible of any of the leadership positions in the club. They should fill in the leadership gaps of the group, not just the president's role, but any responsibility that is not getting done. They should be instrumental in training new members and getting them to fill the open roles in the club leadership.

- **Treasurer** — The Treasurer is in charge of keeping track of the club's budget as well as the budgets for individual events and activities the club puts on. This role is one of the most important to have done properly and one of the least appreciated. Someone who is very detail oriented and can handle keeping track of many numbers is important to this role. The consequence of this role not being done properly can mean you don't have the money to do the events and activities you want to do.

- **Secretary** — This person's role is not only to take notes at meetings, the position can be much more. The secretary should be keeping track of all club documents like room reservations, member sign-in sheets, the constitution and even help the treasurer in keeping track of financial documents. The position can help with logistics including getting refreshments to a meeting or coordinating volunteers.

- **Fundraising** — Many clubs do not have a dedicated fundraising person. They wrap the position into the treasurer, but raising money for the club can be one of the most difficult jobs to do. This person should have a firm grasp of the club finances as well as idea about how the club can make money to help offset the cost of activities. Having one person dedicated to fundraising allows your club to have the funds to do a great recruitment drive, put on exciting events, and bring the club together around a specific goal.

Club Funds

Having money in your club's account helps offset the cost of many miscellaneous expenses associated with having and running a club. Sometimes you want to spend money on food for a social event, or need to make copies of fliers for an event. Where is the money going to come from? It shouldn't be the burden of the club leaders to fork over the money to pay for all the club activities. It is important to have a reliable member of the club managing the finances and making sure that there are as few money problems as possible

Even funds set aside for a specific program in your club should be treated with care. You may have been delegated $300 to put together a booth for the annual fair, but if you can get away with using only $100-200, without sacrificing quality, you should try your best to do so. Someone else might end up needing that funding to make their project a success. Don't waste the money if you can avoid it. Fundraising in clubs can be a very difficult thing to do so don't waste anything.

Fundraising

This section will include explanation and tips on raising money for your club. While feel good fundraising events may boost moral, if they don't effectively generate money for the club they shouldn't be called a fundraiser. To fundraise effectively you need to generate more money then you spend on an event. This could be profit from selling something or just getting donations for a particular activity from fellow students or families in the community.

Fundraising needs to be run proficiently and should make financial sense. Lets say you make $300 from a bake sale, but the total value of all the cooking supplies your club members put in was about $250 and you also make a couple of posters and other visuals that cost money. In this sense your club is no better off than it was before the event even though there is more money in the club coffers. You might as well have just had your club members give you the money they used to purchase materials for the bake sale and saved your time. However, if you can find a way to reduce the cost by perhaps having a baking party the night before and buying the supplies in bulk, that might justify the event. The money needs to make sense to have a successful fundraiser.

1. **Food or product sale**: The primary fundraiser where the club members create something to sell to other students. These can help generate extra money for the club if done properly (if the costs do not exceed the money generated). Be careful not to make club members front the cost and make sure they are reimbursed.

2. **Sponsorship**: For specific events where many other students will attend you can ask local business to sponsor the event which will help generate money for that event. What they are expecting in return is that you mention their contribution and put on the materials that they are a sponsor. Its good for you and good for them.

3. **Donations from other students**: You can ask other students to help raise funds for a specific issue or action. If you want to send your club members to help build affordable housing in a low income community. For example, you can ask other students to pitch in to the fund. This strategy can work well but requires a lot of time investment and more logistics. (See Tabling in Chapter 6)

4. **Door to Door**: Ask members of the community to contribute to your club. This helps when you have a specific activity that you need to raise money for or an issue they can easily understand. Having a great argument and facts to back it up helps a lot.

5. **Funding Boards**: Many schools have committees of administrators or students that have control over a certain amount of funds to distribute between clubs for activities and events. These boards typically have an application process that may involve a face to face interview with the board. Each one usually has a specific focus, whether it is service clubs, student events or outreach activities.

> **Break-Even Events vs. Fun and Visibility**
>
> The primary goal of a fundraising event should be to raise money. However, sometimes you may use a fundraising event to get visibility for your club, which has immeasurable value regardless of the money you raise.

Club Dues

The dues you collect as a club should not be an arbitrary number like $5 per semester, but reflect the amount that the club legitimately need to put on the events and programs they want. The leaders should be able to justify asking the club members for this money and have a reason behind it. The club dues may or may not cover all the club's expected expenses but should be a defined amount. Make sure you're doing your homework by creating a legitimate budget and seeing how much you need.

Tips for Saving Money

1. **Pretend you don't have any**: How would you accomplish your goal with zero funding? You would be very surprised to find out how many things can be done with very few expenses if you really have to.

2. **Get donations from local businesses**: Local businesses are usually willing to contribute some money, food, or store resources to projects and events going on at a campus close by. Always remember to mention their contribution and thank them later!

3. **Reuse old materials**: Sometimes you don't use all of your supplies, posters or other materials from a past project. Design your posters with a fill-in-the-blank date box so you can reuse them for multiple events over the course of the year! You can also make use of equipment that is getting old or out of date by repurposing it for another project.

4. **Put in a little more time**: Frequently you can find a solution by not taking an easy way out, it just takes more effort. This could involve building relationships with other club leaders to communicate what is going on rather than sending a letter or putting out advertisements. Think of something creative.

Mediating Conflicts within your Club

Occasionally conflicts will arise within the club either between members or between the leadership of the group. Any kind of major dispute can seriously threaten the stability and success of the organization. For this reason it is important to be able to identify these problems before they happen and try to find the best possible outcome for the parties involved. These conflicts can become very stressful, so you'll need to keep a cool head and work with both sides to find a solution.

Tips for Mediation:

1. **Get both sides of the story**: Try to understand why each side is having a problem. Talk about this before a meeting between the two parties or at the very beginning of the meeting to get everything out in the open.

2. **Gain both sides' trust**: When a resolution needs to be established you must remain unbiased in your comments and suggestions so that each side can rely on you to properly address their concerns.

3. **Work with each side individually**: Work with the people involved to identify how much they are willing to give to make a resolution happen. When they are isolated from the opposing side they will be more forthcoming and honest about their needs.

4. **Keep your cool**: Success at helping others will depend on your ability to weigh both sides and arbitrate the disagreement in a fair and rational manner. Blowing up or getting emotional will set the discussion back or make a resolution unreachable.

How to Work With your Team

- **Be polite**: Clubs are fun, but you have to get the work done with people from many different backgrounds. Tempers can flare but it's important to stay on everyone's good side as much as possible. If you have a disagreement, resolve it immediately by talking to that person directly then move past it. You still want to be able to have fun and work with that person in the future so ongoing conflicts will make it more stressful.

- **Contribute your ideas**: Be an active part of any debate within the club. Being new to the club just means you have fresh ideas. Everyone in the organization is there to have fun and succeed. Frequently a fresh idea is just what the group needs.

- **Volunteer your time**: Getting things done is in everyone's best interest, so help others as much as you can. Your goals are tied into the success of many people around you as well. You'll share in the success of other activities and you'll be able to ask for their help when you really need it in the future.

- **Deal with slackers**: If someone is not doing what they said they would, try to find out why. You can talk to them directly by approaching the situation in a positive manner: "We all want this event to go off without a hitch, so what part of it are you excited about? How can you use your unique skills to contribute?" Do your best to help motivate them, and try to identify something they would get excited about so they can be part of the team.

- **Learn to disagree**: When you don't have the extra time, or something would adversely affect your project, make sure you say so in a positive way. You'll find that most things can be changed so that everyone can benefit, and it's far better than holding a grudge or sacrificing the quality of your program. Most of the time you just need to make your concerns known.

Starting a New Club

If you have a few friends and a great idea for a club that doesn't exist at your school yet, it may be time to roll up your sleeves and get one started. This is a thrilling experience where you can learn much more about your own leadership abilities than just being in charge of a veteran organization that already has all the rules laid out. Use the following steps to help guide you through the process of starting your very own club, but remember that each school has very different rules and structures for how your organization functions on your campus.

Club Constitution Checklist

1. Introduction/About the Club
2. Goals and Vision
3. Club Structure and Leadership
4. Voting Procedures/ Club Leader Elections
5. How to Amend the Constitution

1. **Check the Rules**: Your school should have an administrative department or designated administrator whose role is to help students form and run their organizations. This could be the Dean of Students, a Director of Clubs & Organizations or a student leadership director. Check with this department or person to see what steps and paperwork you need to fill out to make your club a legitimate and official organization on campus.

2. **Create the Structure**: What function do you want your club to fulfill? Is it going to focus on organizing volunteer projects, mobilizing students into action, or getting students together with a common passion? The answer will help identify what kind of leadership your club will need. For example, if your club is just meeting to talk about philosophy, you may not need a fundraising coordinator unless you foresee the club going on fieldtrips. On the other hand, if you're planning on doing many volunteer projects you may want to create at least one position dedicated to organizing those events. Think through what you want your club to do and create positions and structure to accommodate it. You can use the typical structure at the beginning of the chapter as a template to start with.

3. **Write the constitution**: Once you've established how you want your organization structured and what role you want it to fulfill, you need to write it down in the club constitution. This founding document can give later club leaders and members an idea about the purpose of the organization and can be a reference for how to make decisions and run the club.

4. **Submit Forms/Pay Fees**: Once you've figured out what forms you need to fill out and what fees may be involved, make sure you get them all turned in. Some schools prohibit any official club activities or room reservations until all the paperwork is turned in, so it is essential to complete this task as quickly and completely as possible. You don't want to have a bunch of students ready to come to the meeting only to find out you can't get a room for the group.

5. **Start Recruiting**: Once you have a proper club established you need to have some members. At first you'll need to recruit people to come to the meetings by yourself or with friends. You'll want to have a fair number of people at the first meeting, even if they are your friends because many students wont join a club with no members, it may not be worth their time. (See Recruitment in Chapter 6)

Summary

The roles and structure of the organization contributes to the success of many clubs. Having the appropriate leaders to handle all the issues that come up as well as having an established role for each leader is essential. The role of the fundraiser, which can be one of the most necessary and overlooked jobs, can allow you to put on larger events or better activities with the club. Because fundraising is also one of the most difficult things a club has to do, there are many tips to do it successfully, from selling something to asking for donations or sponsorship. At some point it will become necessary to resolve conflicts within your club or between club members and in this case you need to keep your cool and remain unbiased in order to reach an effective resolution. On occasion you'll want to start a new club that fills a gap in the interests of the college students and you can use the tips in this chapter to help get it started.

Chapter 3: Being a Leader in your Organization

Being a leader is not just a matter of telling people what to do and getting what you want. You'll be required to put in work organizing each project in the background by preparing for meetings and activities. You have a responsibility to make sure things get done, but not to do everything yourself. The skills in this chapter will help with the common tasks you'll face as a leader within your organization.

Time Management

There are only so many hours in the day to get everything done between your studies, friends and club responsibilities. Time management skills will help you to be more effective with the time you have. Its not easy to build more time into your day, but it is important to develop this skill and it takes a lot of mental effort. Decide what is important to accomplish in your day and how much time you will spend on each activity. Planning your time effectively will allow you to know when your free time is, and have more available time.

Measuring Priorities

Efficient vs. Effective: Being efficient means getting a lot of work done in the quickest and most economical way, regardless of the importance of the tasks. Effectiveness on the other hand means getting the tasks done that move you closest to your goal. You could be an efficient person at putting up posters around your campus to advertise for an event. If the original project plan established that the most effective way of reaching your audience was sending out targeted e-mails to other club leaders, then putting up posters may be efficient, but it is not the most effective thing to do. Similarly, creating an intricate filing system for all your incoming e-mails may make you more efficient, but it doesn't help you accomplish anything.

Important vs. Urgent

Important tasks are similar to effective tasks in that they are critical steps that have an impact on your project or event. Your goal should be to spend your time on things that are important and not urgent. This means that you're dealing with key activities, but not at the last minute. If you don't deal with tasks when they're not urgent they can accumulate quickly and force you to deal with them right away, even if it's not convenient to do so.

Deal with items that are not urgent and not important in a disciplined way. Take care of them, but don't spend any more time on them than you have to. This includes tasks like filling out a room reservation for a meeting. Do not ignore these things completely, or they will become urgent and again force you to deal with them at an inconvenient time. You'll end up reacting to things that would have been easier to take care of earlier, like forgetting to reserve the meeting room until the day before and finding out its already booked by someone else.

Multi-tasking is not effective: You'll feel like you're being efficient by getting a lot done at the same time, but it's not the best way to get the most effective tasks done. It may be hard but put down the text-message, close your e-mail and focus on your most important task, get it done quickly and properly then move on to the next task you need to accomplish.

Time Tips:

- Delegate, delegate, delegate. If someone else can do a task, have them do it so you can focus on what only you can do.
- Schedule double the time you think the task will take, but try to get things done in half the time. This allows greater flexibly in your schedule.
- Focus on one of your priorities at a time and work at it until it is finished.
- Know what times of the day and week you work best to maximize your effectiveness.
- Do unpleasant tasks first thing in the morning to avoid putting them off for later in the day or forgetting them entirely.
- Put things on one list, like a to-do list or on a plan you make for your week.
- Keep copies of everything, just in case.
- File important things away immediately.
- Learn to say "no" when you just don't have time.
- Spend some time every day staying organized and at least an hour every week planning out what you need to do.
- Don't schedule every minute – plan time for the unexpected.
- Wear a watch to keep yourself on track and on schedule.

The 100/80/60/40/20 Rule

When planning your week, plan 100% of your time on Monday, 80% of your time on Tuesday, and so on. Things will come up unexpectedly, so you want to leave more time open at the end of the week.

Developing Leaders
Constantly Build the Next Group of Leaders

The goal is to build leaders in your team that are confident and competent at all stages of the year. This will allow you to take on new and challenging projects yourself as they come up. You need to be able to seamlessly pass your job on to someone else so you don't get hung up and stuck in a role you no longer have any interest in. This basic concept of leadership development ensures that you continue to build leaders in your group by allowing them to grow and take on different parts of your job. Eventually they will replace your original position while you move into a different role.

Dividing Roles and Responsibilities

Dividing up roles allows everyone to contribute to the success of the project by being in charge of their own distinct parts. Identify the best roles for members of your team based on their unique skills. Each person responds to leadership styles and practices differently so keep that in mind when distributing tasks.

Assigning roles to your team:

- **Specialization**: Each person can become an expert in a particular element of the project. The goal is that they become the best person at doing that job by spending their time perfecting the role. For example, one member of your team could handle meeting with leaders of other clubs and going to their meeting so that they build a relationship and know everyone.

What if you like your job?

It should always be your goal to do tasks better and more effectively, but how can you do that when you're bogged down in the mundane parts of your job. Getting other people involved and participating will give you more time to make those improvements.

- **Sense of Ownership**: By giving a member of your team responsibility over one aspect of the project, you allow them to become invested in its success. They'll be engaged in the project because they are making their own decisions and taking ownership of their responsibilities. Plus, you wont have to tell them what to do all the time.

- **Work is Distributed**: A collaborative team will accomplish more than one person managing each person's tasks and handing out work that needs to get done. The primary leader will still have organizational work to do but the team will already know what they are responsible for and what they need to keep track of.

- **Reduced Stress**: You won't have to worry as much about the small and relatively unimportant tasks getting done because they should be handled by the individuals in their respective roles. Each team member is worrying about their particular element and the team leader can focus on the overall problems and pushing the project forward.

Steps for Building New Leaders:

1. Begin training new club members and volunteers in your specific project or the club in general with the basic leadership skills.

2. Promote the most active team member into team leader positions and help them train the group, slowly allowing them to teach more and more of the material.

3. As their skill and confidence grows, continue to train them and challenge their abilities.

4. Delegate parts of your responsibilities to them until multiple people have taken over various aspects of your role.

5. Now its time to work on the next project or program: plan it out, recruit people for it, and then organize yourself out of it again.

Organizing a Training

1. **Prepare**: Creating a training program should be a task of its own. You'll want to become well versed in the topic you are teaching. Use the topics in this manual as a guideline. Bring in other sources for more in depth training on a specific topic.

2. **Bring materials**: Give your trainees something to take with them so they can reference it later. You'd be surprised at how long people hold onto good notes.

3. **Make it interactive**: When you are presenting the material ask for feedback, answers to questions, and examples from the audience. Using an appropriate example gives people a reason to listen because they may be able to directly use elements of the training in the real world. They will learn and retain more information when they are engaged in the training.

4. **Break into groups**: Have an activity as part of the training that forces individuals to use what they've just learned in a theoretical scenario. It makes them think through what you've taught them so far and if they discover they don't understand something as well as they thought, they can ask for clarification later. For example, if you're teaching them how to plan a project, give them a sample tabling event to plan in groups.

5. **Keep it short**: Trainings should be on one subject at a time, and no longer than an hour. Any longer than that and people become tired and retain less information.

Running an Effective Meeting

A great meeting helps to build a stronger team through effective discussion and debate. Achieving an agreement about the correct course of action gives each person a sense of direction about the project. It can also serve to share information rapidly with many people and brainstorm new ideas. On the other end of the spectrum, meetings that are agonizingly unstructured and off track to the point where very little is accomplished can severely hurt a project. No one enjoys them and it becomes a time wasting activity. This is why it is so important to make the meetings a good use of time and an effective part of accomplishing your goals.

Even for a weekly club meeting it is important to make sure things are well organized and under control. The environment may be more fun and relaxed but the club leaders are still responsible for everything running smoothly. You still want to hit your goals for the meeting, whether it is a discussion about what charity to volunteer with in the coming weeks, or figuring out where to do your favorite activity. Most people don't want the business part of the meeting to degenerate into social time without anything being decided. Keep everything moving and keep to the agenda.

The Secret to Keeping on Track

Set times next to each agenda item with how long the group should spend on that topic. Be realistic because you're going to need to stick to the schedule for the most part. This lets you know when it's time to move on and focuses the conversation on only the most important topics, rather than getting sidetracked on unimportant matters.

Setting Agenda Priorities

- **Think about your goals**: What is the reason you need to have a meeting and how will this get you closer to your goals? Think ahead about how this fits into future plans. Remember, there is no point in having a meeting if it doesn't get you closer to your goal by accomplishing something. If you just want to socialize, make it a social activity rather than a meeting.

- **Generating Action**: For a meeting to be productive there needs to be some action generated. Plan on delegating out tasks during the meeting and setting a timeline to ensure things are completed in a timely manner after the meeting is done.

- **Participation and Delegation**: Group participation is a must for effective meetings. Have every member of your group speak about a section of the meeting so that everyone gets a chance to contribute to the meeting. This helps develop new leaders by building confidence and group unity. Meeting facilitators should only talk about a quarter of the time and mainly just to move the agenda along.

- **Keeping on Time**: Put times next to each item on the agenda to make sure everyone in the meeting knows when its time to move on.

Guidelines for the meeting

- **Preparation for the meeting**: Spend as much time preparing for the meeting as the meeting is set to last. Ask yourself questions like: Is the location of the room convenient? Is the room big enough? Is it set up for discussion? Do you have a whiteboard for brainstorming? Sign-in contact sheet? All the necessary materials? Refreshments for socializing? Set and generally agreed upon agenda?

- **Know your goals**: The agenda should clearly lay out the goals for the meeting and establish an atmosphere that makes everyone comfortable. Figure out what discussions need to happen and what decisions need to be made.

- **Prepare all participants**: Everyone coming to the meeting should have a basic sense of the goals, how they will participate and who else will be in attendance. Meeting facilitators should have a sense of what needs to come out of the meeting and who is best suited to do each task so that they can guide the conversation.

- **Anticipate the problems**: The most difficult part of running a successful meeting is dealing with the dynamics of the attendees. The meeting facilitator needs to be encouraging discussion, laying out summarized opinions clearly, as well as making people feel comfortable enough to talk.

  ### Club Meeting Quirks

  - Some people just don't want to talk. They just want to listen and hang out.
  - The goal of the club meeting could be to talk about the one thing everyone has in common. It is still a goal, just not as tangible as planning an event.

- **Put goals in context**: While most people in the meeting will have some grasp of the purpose of the meeting, it's always good to reiterate why everyone is there. Put the goal of the meeting and any major issues into context of the larger picture so the newer people know what's going on. This is a great way to reenergize everyone.

- **Plan some social time:** Many people join clubs so they can hang out with other people who share their interests and passions. For club meeting especially, make sure that something social is built into the meetings so everyone can have some fun while getting stuff done.

- **Recap after the meeting**: Take a few minutes after the agenda wraps up to talk casually with the people who were in the meeting and ask what worked and didn't work well. Use these pros and cons to decide what to change for the next meeting.

- **Follow up after the meeting**: In case tasks and activities were delegated to group members, check in a short while after the meeting: thank people for volunteering and make sure delegated tasks are happening. This is essential to keep things moving outside the meeting.

Simple Legislative & Parliamentary Procedures

At times your club may need to make official and binding decisions rather than the casual decision making process your club normally uses. This can include voting in new officers, major financial decisions or other decisions that require a specific vote count to be taken. For the most part these decisions are made using a form of parliamentary procedures which ensures that the meeting can be run effectively and legitimately. Having a specific set of rules to govern who can speak and when motions can be brought up for debate helps to guarantee that everyone gets a chance to speak and that the meeting proceeds in an orderly fashion. Parliamentary procedure can become quite complex and only a brief explanation based on Roberts Rules of Order Newly Revised will be included here. Typically the specific rules for voting and decision making will be found in your club constitution and you can use whatever combination of rules you feel is appropriate for your group.

Terms

- **Bylaws**: These are the rules that govern the decision making group to ensure that all procedures are set before an important decision is made and that everyone knows the same rules.

- **Minutes**: This is a written record of the meeting and should include motions, vote totals and the major arguments made during the meeting.

- **Quorum**: Is the number of members that must be present at the meeting for any substantial decisions to be made. This ensures that business may proceed despite a certain number of absentees, as long as the minimum number is reached. This number can typically be found in the bylaws for the organization.

- **Chair**: This is the presiding officer of the meeting. He or she is chosen to keep the meeting in order, take motions and determine the order of the debate. This person is typically a facilitator of the meeting, but may vote in accordance with the bylaws.

- **Motion**: A motion is a suggested action or request made by a member of the board after obtaining the recognition of the chair.These are agreed as statements with a common meaning that every member of the board knows and understands. Motions typically proceed as requested unless there is an objection, where a vote will be required for the motion to proceed.

Typical Order of the Meeting:

1. Call the meeting to order
2. Review and approval of the past meeting minutes
3. Approval of the meeting agenda
4. Unfinished business from the previous meeting
5. New business to be discussed at the current meeting
6. Committee reports
7. Officer reports
8. Announcements and Adjournment

Types of Voting

Unanimous Consent: This method passes a motion with unanimous approval without a vote count unless there is an objection. In the case of an objection a different type of vote will be required. Acclamation, or unanimous consent, is typically used for simple votes on non-confrontational topics.

Roll Call: All members will be required to vote yes or no without abstentions and their specific choice will be recorded with their name. Typically voting will go around the room and each member may pass either once or twice before they are required to submit their final vote.

Majority: This is a set amount of the members currently in attendance that are required to vote in favor of the motion either by standing up, raising their hands, submitting a ballot or some other way of indicating their vote choice. The most common is a simple majority, where the required vote is just over 50% of attendance. Another type is a 2/3rds vote for more important votes like changing the constitution or bylaws.

Making Amendments

Person A: "I move to amend the current proposal so that the section that currently reads ___ will be changed to read ___." Stating the section to be changed and how it will be changed allows all members to follow along and be clear about the change.

Chair: "All those in favor of amending the section that reads ___ to ___? All those opposed? Abstaining?" The chair restates the amendment and calls for a vote.

Standard Motions and Order of Debate:

Person A: "I move that ___" and clearly phrase your recommended course of action, proposed motion, or request.

Person B: "Second" to agree with the motion put forth.

Chair: "The proposal on the floor is to ___." The chair restates the proposal so that everyone can clearly hear and understand.

Person A: "I move to debate current proposal for ___ minutes." This moves the proposal into the debating stage and puts a cap on extraneous and unimportant discussions. Each persons speaking time can also be set at this time.

Person B: "Second"

Chair: "Debate is open on the current proposal for ___ minutes." Without objections the debate is open. The chair may create a list of members who wish to speak on the issue.

- Debate proceeds until time has been reached. During this time members can speak, amendments can be proposed and voted on, and additional motions can be made such as extending or ending debate time. -

Chair: "Time is up. Are there any motions on the floor?" This lets everyone know that another motion is needed to move the meeting along.

Person A: "I move to call this proposal to question." This proposes a vote on the current proposal. If you have a special request for a type of voting you should also specify that in the motion.

Person B: "Second."

Chair: "The proposal to ___ has been called to a vote. All those in favor ___?" The chair instructs the group how to indicate their choice (hand raise, ballot, etc).

Chair "All those opposed? Abstaining?"

Chair: "The proposal passes (or fails). The results are ___ for, ___ against, and ___ abstaining." State the results so all members know and so that it can be recorded in the minutes.

Chair: "Are there any other motions on the floor? The next order of business is ___" The chair opens the floor to any other requests before proceeding to the next point on the agenda.

Basic Motions and Uses

	Requires Recognition	Requires a Second	Debatable	Amendable	Vote Required	May be Reconsidered
Adjourn	Y	Y	N	N	Majority	N
Recess	Y	Y	N	Y	Majority	N
Limit or Extend Debate	Y	Y	N	Y	2/3rds	Y
Postpone	Y	Y	Y	Y	Majority	Y
Refer to a committee	Y	Y	Y	Y	Majority	Y
Amend	Y	Y	Y	Y	Majority	Y
General Motions	Y	Y	Y	Y	Majority	Y
Reconsider Previous Motion	N	Y	Y	N	Majority	N
Override Committee Decision	Y	Y	Y	Y	2/3rds or Majority	Only negative votes
Requests (Inquires, Procedure, Urgent non business problems)	N	N	N	N	---	N
Suspend the Normal Rules	N	N	N	N	2/3rds	N
Withdraw a Motion	Y	Y	N	N	Majority	Only negative votes
Objection to Consideration	N	N	N	N	2/3rds	Only negative votes

Summary

Developing the skills you need to be a leader in your role in the club is at the core of this chapter. Managing your time effectively can mean the difference between accomplishing your goals or getting bogged down in irrelevant, time consuming activities. You can also boost the effectiveness of your project by identifying and completing the most important tasks first as well as delegating tasks to other members of your team. These tactics require more effort on your part but help generate more of an effect in the end by freeing up your time and getting the important things done quickly. Additionally, the ability to run meetings in an effective manner is an important skill to develop because most of the action for your group will be generated as a result of meetings.

Chapter 4: Get the Word Out with Messaging, Advertising, and News Media

At some point in time you'll need to tell the student body about the project you're working on or about your club's activities. A great idea without the support of great communication skills will not get very far. By using these techniques to get the word out you'll be able to create a winning message to grab people's attention with a variety of advertising methods and media attention. This can help bring new members into your club or get people out to an event.

Creating an Engaging Message

Whether it is a great guest speaker or getting students to volunteer, you need to reach people who are not paying attention. Creating a good message will help you custom tailor ideas of your project be the most effective in reaching your target groups. The ideal

> **Structuring a quick action statement**
> 1. Present the Problem
> 2. Propose the Solution
> 3. Explain how your target group can help

message will get your target's attention by focusing the what makes your event different and the benefits of taking that action. Avoid statements that state the similarities your event shares with other events because you don't need to reiterate what someone will already assume about your activity. You can also use your knowledge about the other activities going on around campus to think of creative methods to present your message.

> **Double Check for Jargon**: Always have someone outside of the team check your message. Advertising campaigns have fallen drastically short of expectations because people couldn't understand the message.

Steps to Message Crafting:

1. **Defining your issue or event**: What is your vision for your project? What is the objective? Why does it matter?

2. **Defining the audience**: What is the main audience you're trying to attract to your program and why? Who will benefit from your actions? Who is this message directed at: Students, the news media, a school administrator?

3. **Connect with your target's interests**: What are the interests of your target group? Focus on specific qualities of your issue but also include general needs that require their attention like school work or paying rent, depending on what you're trying to communicate.

4. **Identify things competing for the target's attention**: Who and what are the competitors for their attention and time? Include all that come to mind like other activities, work, school.

5. **Similarities to other events**: What qualities make your issue or event similar to others going on. These are things that people will expect from the category of events or issues you're working on so you don't even have to mention them. Example: you don't need to mention there is going to be music at a concert.

6. **Recognize What's Different**: What aspect makes your activity different than activities that are going on around campus. How is it different from what people will assume about your project?

7. **Identify Unique Benefits**: What are the best benefits of your project, issue or event. This includes the strongest points from the previous steps. Present a solution to the target while mentioning what makes the solution special. Identify the unique benefits. This gives you a basic and strong statement you can use as a template for your messaging. Alter the message to suit your needs as different situations arise.

Sample Message Craft
Example: Multicultural Festival

1. **Defining the issue**: Students at our school should be **exposed a variety of cultures from around the world**. The goal is to invite all the different cultural clubs on campus to set up an area of the fair to **represent their distinct cultural identity**.

2. **Defining the audience**: The targets will be the **students not affiliated with the cultural organizations** on campus. These students will benefit from this event by learning more about other people.

3. **Connect with your target's interests**: Specifically to this campaign, the students are looking for something **fun and engaging** to participate in. Other needs include satisfying **being fed and socializing** with other students.

4. **Identify things competing for the target's attention**: College students are being pulled by the requirements of their **classes, homework, work, and other social activities**.

5. **Similarities to other events**: This is a club festival at its roots. People will be expecting many **different clubs** to be there with **displays at their tables**.

6. **Recognize what's different**: This event is different because it involves areas where clubs can set up a **scene or environment** that other students can **interact with the club members**.

7. **Identify unique benefits**: This event will benefit the students by **exposing them to other cultures** in a **fun and engaging way**, allowing them to **feel what it's like in other countries**. The **food and displays** will let the club show off their **unique cultural identity**.

Messaging Missteps:

You may have the best of intentions when trying to use powerful elements to define your message, but the following are examples of errors that can occur. Sometimes they just don't make sense.

- **Organization Lingo** — Ex: Mentioning SAIC, an acronym for the campaign that most people are unfamiliar with.

- **Unrelated Statements** — Ex: Making an analogy to the civil rights movement during a campaign for a new events center.

- **Words & Phrases Associated with other things** — Claiming that the administration is waterboarding the students by excluding them from participating in the academic board meetings.

- **Boring or Passive Words** — Ex: This idea is good because professors can hear what students have to say, which makes them better teachers and so students can get a good education.

Getting Your Project Noticed: Visibility
Advertising Campaigns

Ad campaigns let people know about what is going on around campus. Advertising is used to tell people about events going on and ways they can get more information. It is nearly impossible to generate any action with passive visibility, such as telling people to call into a local politician to influence his or her vote on an education issue, but you can remind them of the date and time of an event they were planning to go to.

Putting up posters is the most traditional method for advertising on college campuses. Most school have designated areas full of posters about all the events going on. This makes it important that you come up with creative ways to get your message out to your target groups. Consider whether the specific method you choose is cost effective. How many people are going to get the message for every dollar (or hour) you spend on the advertising method?

There is a trade-off between the time investment in creating the type of advertising, the monetary cost, and the audience it will be seen by. This is the difference between coming up with a creative idea that takes a lot of labor and time investment but doesn't cost a lot of money versus spending a large amount of money to have someone design and print a flier or poster that gets done quickly and easily. An example would be hand drawing murals on posters – each poster takes an extremely long time to create, which limits the number of people who will see it, although it does draw more attention than the average poster.

Making Use of Color Schemes and Thematic Elements

Creating a unified color scheme gets your advertising recognized more often than others. If people begin to see a set of similar red posters in a sea of grey or white posters they will begin to notice that your ads stand out. The goal of having a unified theme is that student will associate the repeated visuals with your message.

It helps if you can create a theme that flows through your advertising campaign that people will identify with your issue or event. This could be an iconic figure, a Viking for example, or some specific and unique image you want to associate with your initiative. The best theme will be easily recognizable and be able to communicate your message in visual form. Keep it simple. You want people to make quick links between your message and your theme.

Another method uses references or associations with popular brands, like car companies or corporations, and pop culture, like popular movies or public figures. This is less recommended, as your ad campaign then becomes dependent on the popularity of the brand you choose. However, you may not be able to use it because of copyright laws. It's best to check before using an existing brand as inspiration.

Estimated Cost Per View:

Online: <$0.01

Posters: $0.04

Fliers: $0.10

Newspaper: $0.18

T-Shirts: $0.30

Design Tips

When you are designing any kind of visual advertisement, from posters to fliers to e-mails, keep in mind these basic principles.

- **The Visual Grab**: The grab gives the viewer a reason to keep looking and learning more. This could be your eye catching image, a captivating slogan, or unique color that draws people's attention to the advertisement.

- **Visual Order Matters**: What do you want to be noticed first? This could be something that your target group will pay attention to and keep reading where others won't. It's typically the slogan and visual. Once you've got someone reading make sure they see things in the proper order. Place elements from top to bottom or left to right, but also arrange the design by font size and visuals.

- **Don't Jump Around**: Make it as easy as possible for the viewer to read what you want to communicate. Keep it simple and ordered. Don't put the time and date of an event in visual order before the statement saying what the event is, because people will lose track in the split second they glance at the poster.

- **Be Unique**: Nothing hurts your advertising campaign like being completely average and thus, unnoticeable. Strive to make your campaign stand out. Go through the message crafting again to come up with ideas.

Active Visibility Events

Events with the sole purpose of making someone aware of an issue or event have a specific set of rules to follow. This can be used to publicize an event, make people aware of an issue or show off your club's specialty. (See Tabling for more info on logistics of visibility events)

- **Make Yourself Stand Out**: Nothing generates attention like screaming for it. You want to be noticeable, so use bright colors, unique images, or something out of the ordinary like having someone playing an acoustic guitar in front of your table. Make sure to reinforce a positive impression of your event or campaign.

- **Visibility Events Need Visuals**: Draw the attention of both students and media to your cause through striking visuals. This could be a prop that has a unique connection with the issue or event, like a giant walking textbook for a textbooks affordability issue or everyone dressed in Halloween costumes while advertising for the annual campus Halloween festival.

- **Be Active**: Drawing attention is difficult, so the more excited and energized you and your volunteers are the better everything will look. Talk to people face to face rather than sitting behind a table, have people move around to make the event more exciting.

Types of Advertising Methods

Ways to Boost Visibility		
Try a different shape: Make posters round, or triangular, or even blob-like. It doesn't matter what shape it is as long as it stands out.	**Use a unique color:** Nobody else is using fuchsia posters? If your event or issue won't suffer from being associated with bright pink then go for it.	**Print glossy posters:** If you get your posters professionally printed they'll stand out against hand-made posters and they'll convey the image of legitimacy and size
Professionalism helps: The more legitimate the flier looks, the more someone is going to take the time to look at it. This includes using card stock, glossy printing, well designed messages and visuals.	**Keep it simple:** Only include relevant information and stick to your message. The longer it is the less it will be read it.	**Hand it out at relevant functions:** Get to your core audience quickly by selecting appropriate locations like club meetings or relevant events.
Catchy without color: Most ads appear in black and white, so think of an interesting grab that will work without color. You need your ad to stand out against other ads and the standard newspaper content.	**Make a deal:** Work out a deal with your campus newspaper for ideal ad placement and a potential discount.	**Take out a whole page:** A whole page makes your ad unavoidable. It is usually more expensive and is only reserved for once or twice a year at best.
Designate event or project staff: T-shirts can be useful to identify the students in charge so people can ask them questions.	**Double your views:** Remember that T-shirts are two sided, so take advantage of getting views from both directions.	**Unified color scheme:** Make the t-shirts the same unique color to make them catchy. Students will associate the different parts of the advertising together.
Be straight and to the point: Keep your message concise despite having more space for your message. Don't beat around the bush, people will just ignore the message.	**Use relevant mailing lists or groups:** Sending an e-mail to an appropriate mailing list or group will boost the number of people who read the message.	**Start an interest group:** Create a group specifically for your event or issue so you know everyone in it is interested.

Type	Description	Pros	Cons
Posters	~Butcher paper posters colored with markers, photocopied ads, or glossy professionally printed posters.	~It's simple, easy to produce and relatively cheep. ~You tend to get a large amount of views per dollar because of the volume of students walking by.	~Students see them but don't pay attention because there are so many. ~Its hard to reach your specific target because everyone is exposed to the poster.
Fliers	~Small informational papers passed out individually ~Anything from informational pamphlets to basic info about an event	~Cheep and easy to mass produce. ~It gets into students' hands	~Student will throw it away without looking at it especially when other groups are handing out fliers too. ~Causes litter that is difficult to pick up.
News Ads	~Advertising space in your school newspaper.	~You can reach a large number of students at one time.	~Even a small ad can cost a lot ~You can't control placement. ~People will not necessarily see it.
T-Shirts	~Inform people by letting them read the shirt as they are walking around or sitting in class	~Students see it in addition to/ instead of posters. ~You can bring into class. ~If someone is interested they can ask for more info.	~They are almost prohibitively expensive for mass advertising: 20-30 shirts can cost hundreds of dollars.
Online	~Using methods like e-mail, websites, and instant messenger to communicate with other students (See Online Communications)	~Free advertising through mailing lists, target website ads and networking websites. ~Groups on networking sites get you to your targets	~Any form of online communication can be dismissed easily. It's difficult to ensure that people will see it.

Generating Media Attention

The media is an incredibly powerful tool. If you can master media relations it will help achieve your goals, reach out to allies, recruit supporters, let the student body know what is going on, or get a movement going around your issues. The news media can give you a lot of free visibility and can boost the image of your event or campaign.

Elements of a good media plan: (See Message Crafting)

1. **Keep it simple**: Short and direct is the key when creating a media message. Print and TV news reporters are always short on time so communicate your event and message in as few sentences as possible. They are far more likely to listen that way.

2. **Grab their attention**: Differentiate your story from all the other stories that news reporters are hearing about. Give them a reason to pursue what you have to say. Figure out what makes your event or campaign unique and communicate it.

3. **Timeliness:** Your story needs to be presented as an urgent problem in order to get their attention. Communicate that sense of urgency in order to generate the story when you need it. This is the reason they'll pursue your story now rather than forgetting about it because it happens months from now.

4. **Photo Op**: A picture is worth a thousand words and media professionals love good visuals to connect with their stories, especially involving TV or print stories.

I don't need the news to cover this... The Myth about the Media

The news media is a great ally to have on your side no matter what you're working on. They can pave the way to your success or leave your issues stuck in the mud. Even if you don't think you need media coverage to push your campaign forward, it never hurts to submit a celebratory piece to the paper so that students at your school can simply know what is going on around campus and the interesting stuff

Steps to Getting Media Attention

1. **Create or find a major action event to generate a story**: Reporters like action. Use your event or a related event to spring board your issue or event into the press' attention. Ex: "In conjunction with the school administration announcing it's commitment to ensuring the mental health of all students the Psychology Club will be hosting a luncheon between the school administration, the psychology department and interested students…"

2. **Creating your materials**

    a. **Create a media list (newspapers, TV news, radio, magazines, blogs)**: Include the station, type of media, contact reporter if possible, phone, fax, and e-mail.

    b. **Write a Press Advisory**: This is the press' invitation to your event so make it catchy and engaging. Make this sound like a "can't miss" event.

    c. **Write a Press Release**: This is the ideal story you'd like them to publish. They'll use a lot of the material and information you provide in the press release in their article.

    d. **Questions and Answers**: Write out any and all questions you think reporters will ask. Attach answers to each one based off your message, press advisory and release. This keeps everything consistent.

Timeline for Media:

One Week before, 8am-9am:

  Submit Press Advisory

  First round media calls

Two days before, 8am-9am:

  Second round press advisory

  Second round media calls

Day of, before the event:

  Third round press advisory

Day of, after the event:

  Submit Press Release

  Follow-up media calls

Day after, 8am-9am

  Contact unreached media outlets

3. **Submitting a Press Advisory**: Submit the press advisory by fax and e-mail one week before the action event is to take place to give the reporters plenty of time to put it in their schedules. Send it again two days before the event and again the morning of. Send it early in the morning, between 8am and 9am. They'll see it before they get distracted with other deadlines later in the day.

4. **Contacting the Media**: Call immediately following your submission of the press advisory. Give them a brief overview of the event and ask if they received the advisory. It puts it on their radar and differentiates your fax from all the other ones coming in. Also do a follow up call two days before the event and the morning of. Again, contact members of the press between 8am and 9am.

5. **Follow-up Communication and Press Release**: Follow up with both the reporters that attended the event and especially the ones who didn't. Just because they didn't come doesn't mean they aren't interested, they may just have been busy. This follow-up should include answering any additional questions they may have and asking about their desire to publish the story. Be insistent!

6. **Build a relationship with the press**: Establishing a relationship with members of the press can be a great benefit and will help get positive coverage in the future. If you keep providing them with interesting stories to cover they'll be grateful.

Avoid the Worst Press

Be Careful: Sometimes reporters will try to bait you into saying something you shouldn't so they can write their own version of the story. Pay attention to why they are asking certain questions.

Stay on Message: Keep to your message no matter what. If a reporter asks an odd question, answer it in a way that draws the answer back into the topic of the event without giving away any compromising quotes.

Mind your Surroundings: If reporters are around don't talk about anything other than the event or the subject of the event. Don't let them quote you saying something potentially inappropriate.

What happens when there is a car chase at the same time as your event?

Despite your best efforts, sometimes no one will come to a press event and sometimes your stories just won't get covered. There are a lot of other events going on at the time. Just try again next time.

Press Advisory

University of Colorado, Colorado Springs

Conservation Students of Colorado

NEWS ADVISORY

FOR IMMEDIATE RELEASE: CONTACT:

Monday, May 5, 2008, 10 AM MT   Jim Jackson, 468-648-9658, jjackson@uccs.edu
Michelle Nguyen, 468-863-9782, mnguyen@uccs.edu

CONSERVATION CONCERT SEEKS TO URGE UCCS CAMPUS TO GO GREEN

UCCS Conservation Students of Colorado puts on a concert with local bands and campus speakers to lobby school administrators to use solar energy to help power the campus

WHO: Jameson Dow, Professor, Head of the Environmental Analysis Department, UCCS

Paula Sheen, Executive Vice President, UCCS Student Government Association

Emilio Martinez, Conservation Students of Colorado, UCCS Chapter

Student Bands - Sewer Monkeys, The Scribes, Advocates of Indecision

WHAT: The Conservation Students of Colorado is partnering with the University of Colorado, Colorado Springs Student Government Association to put on a concert to rally support for solar energy on campus. Thousands of UCCS students are expected to attend to hear the music, visit the booths advocating for various environmental issues, and eat food being sold by campus organizations. The Conservation Concert seeks to put pressure on Chancellor Miller to take action on making the campus more environmentally sustainable by implementing a policy to put solar panels on roofs of new and existing buildings on campus.

WHEN: 12:00pm – 3:30pm, Thursday, May 15th

WHERE: On the steps of the University Center, University of Colorado, Colorado Springs {Directions: Take Austin Bluffs Parkway towards the UCCS campus and turn into Parking Lot 3. Use the visitor parking spaces. Signs will guide you to the University Center}

VISUALS: Thousands of students will be gathered at the steps the University Center to hear the concert and speakers. 15 booths will also fill the area selling food and providing informational materials.

More information can be found at www.uccs.edu/SGA/ConservationConcert

###

{Put your logo or letterhead here}

NEWS ADVISORY

FOR IMMEDIATE RELEASE:
[Date advisory sent to press]

CONTACT: [Full Name, Phone #, E-mail]

[Catchy headline]

[Subtitle explaining the headline]

WHO: [List prominent speakers, participants and organizations taking part]

WHAT: [2-3 descriptive sentences about the event]

WHEN: [Date and time of event]

WHERE: [Where the event will take place. Include brief but descriptive directions for anyone to get there and where to park]

VISUALS: [Describe exciting photo ops for the press, anything relevant they can take a picture of or shoot video footage of]

More information can be found at [website address].

[Indicates end of message]

Press Release

Campus Culture Clash

Ohio State University

NEWS RELEASE

FOR IMMEDIATE RELEASE: CONTACT:

Monday October 20th, 9 AM CT   Patrick Cooper, 614-212-5972
pcooper@osu.edu

Jeanette Millman, 614-556-9110,
jmillman@osu.edu

CAMPUS CULTURE CLASH FESTIVAL HELPS NEEDY FAMILIES

OSU cultural clubs band together to organize a festival dedicated to helping community families who have hit hard times.

The Campus Culture Clash organization at Ohio State University, representing a wide array of students from different cultures organized a festival on campus to raise money, collect donations of toys and canned foods, and raise awareness about the plight of the homeless in the region. The organization put together a multi-day series of events, music and booths where students could find ways to help alleviate the problem in their community.

"I think it's terrible the number of homeless individuals just in the neighborhoods around OSU. This is something we really need to fix," said Mary Martinez, a concerned student.

The Community Service Club at Ohio State University for example regularly holds events where their members volunteer with local soup kitchens, homeless shelters, and community support organizations and they see first hand the risk that many families face when they are barely scraping by to make ends meat. Emily Johnson, president of the Community Service Club was excited to hear that other organizations were beginning to recognize this problem and take action.

"We really wanted to organize something where we could give back to our community and show that no matter what our cultural backgrounds are or what differences we have, we can all come together to help the less fortunate in our community," Student Chair of Campus Culture Clash, Mike Nguyen said.

OSU Director of Community Relations Kathy Bellevue commends Campus Culture Clash for creating a provocative event that really hit home with students on campus, "When people heard the homeless rate around our campus was at 3-4%, it seemed like they were very eager to help and donate whatever they could."

[Your logo or letterhead]

NEWS RELEASE

FOR IMMEDIATE RELEASE:

[Date release sent to press]

CONTACT:

[Full Name, Phone #, E-mail]

[Full Name, Phone #, E-mail]

[Headline, short and descriptive]

[Subtitle explaining the headline]

[Describe the event that just happened with a brief explanation of why its significant]

[Include a quote from a supportive student or community member explaining the situation]

[Personal story about the event including a short quote]

[Quote and explanation about the event from your organization. Describe what action needs to be taken or why the action is justified]

[Include an additional explanation or outline information as needed]

50

In a recent report compiled by the Student Advocacy Organization of Ohio, homeless rates have doubled over the last twenty years. This report found that children account for more than one quarter of all homeless individuals.

"We've collected about $11,000 in contributions from students, faculty and community members so far, as well as boxes and boxes of canned food and hygiene supplies," Campus Culture Clash Event Coordinator Alex Louis said. "This event was amazingly successful with a huge outpouring of support from our community. There is still a lot of work to be done but if its anything like this event we're going to continue to be able to help the less fortunate members of our community."

The Campus Culture Clash is planning to organize at least one more festival for the end of the school year to try to break their fundraising record and help raise even more supplies and money for local charities. They are planning on bringing many more clubs on board for the next event and get additional sponsorship and support from local businesses.

The next event is tentatively scheduled for early next April.

More information can be found at http://www.osu.edu/clubs/CCC

The Campus Cultural Clash is an umbrella organization representing the members of the diverse cultural organization at Ohio State University, and is responsible for organizing events and bringing together all the different cultures of the school and communicating with the community around campus in Columbus.

[Explain telling statistics to back up the story]

[Additional straight and to the point quote to summarize the initiative/action]

[What your organization is doing to continue the initiative/action]

More information can be found at [website address for organization or campaign].

[Describe your organization in one sentence]

[Indicates end of message]

Summary

Effectively communicating your ideas and issues will go great lengths towards reaching your goals. The first step is creating a message that will communicate the core ideas of your program in a concise manner and allow you to make use of thematic elements to help boost visibility. Once you've identified your message you can begin to strategize about how best to communicate that message, through using different types of advertising campaigns like posters, fliers, newspaper ads, t-shirts and on-line mechanisms, or using the news media to get the word out. Your campus newspapers can be a great way to communicate with the student body. Cultivate your relationship with members of the press and provide them with easy opportunities to generate stories that you need to create a successful program.

Chapter 5: Getting Connected and Building a Coalition

Sometimes, your own club will not have access to all the volunteers, skills or people you need to achieve you goals. It helps to bring in other people and groups to help facilitate your goals and to help them achieve theirs. This way you can pool your resources with other clubs to be even more successful than before.

Coalition Building

Getting students involved from different facets of the campus is a way to get the depth and breadth of experience you need when organizing an issue campaign or a major event. This adds to your ability to mobilize volunteers, get the word out to interested parties and boost the image of the event. For example, if you want to partner with a few other academic organization to start a job fair, together you may have the knowledge and connections to get it done.

Steps for Building a Coalition

1. **Identify your allies**: Figure out which organizations or school departments would benefit from participating and which ones you feel would contribute the most to your success.

2. **Figure out roles**: Similar to the way you identify who on your team would best be able to handle certain projects, figure out which of your allies you'd ideally like to have take on parts of the project.

3. **Meet to brainstorm**: Brainstorming is a great way to get people invested in an event or campaign because each person and organization is coming up with ideas and contributing to the overall image of the project.

4. **Make the coalition collaborative**: After you've met with the groups once or twice you can begin to build an organizational structure to identify each of the group's roles and determine how decisions are made for the coalition.

Lobbying Your Student Government

At some point you may need to work with your school's student government organization, to work on a project you're really passionate about. Student government's have a large amount of resources and connections relative to most other school organizations. You could be asking for funding, or trying to get a new policy adopted on campus. To this end, you'll need to convince the members of your student government about the value of your request and get people on your side. You can also use many of these tips to lobby your local elected representatives if your issue or campaign has some impact in the local community.

Tips for lobbying success

1. **Build a personal connection**: Make an effort to introduce yourself to legislative decision makers. A personal connection goes a long way towards getting someone to listen to the benefits of your proposal. Take the time to ask them about other issues you are working on to get a feel for their response.

2. **Do you research**: You may have a friend or acquaintance in student government who can give you some pointers about who to talk to and where people stand. Use your contacts to do research on where your initiative might get hung up. Know which pros and cons of your issue they will bring up or which ones will most effectively convince them. Going in with the facts is indispensable.

3. **Talk to decision makers in person**: Discuss your issue with them and see what concerns they have. Take those opinions into account when you want to pass a proposal. You may not decide to address their concerns, but at least you'll be prepared for their arguments.

4. **Identify elite decision makers**: Many elected officials listen to an influential member of the legislative council or student government. Get these people on your side, they tend to be able to influence more votes than just their individual contribution. Don't get on the bad side of the elite decision makers because their influence may be enough to kill your initiative in its tracks.

5. **Be prepared**: Once you've gotten a feel for the political climate around a certain issue, ensure you have enough confirmed votes to pass your initiative before it is brought up for a vote. This way you'll limit the degree to which the vote could turn unexpectedly against you.

6. **Have an ally**: If you don't know a member of the decision making board find one strong ally to champion your cause. This person must be able to clearly articulate the nuances of your initiative and know where it can and cannot be compromised.

Networking

Networking is about building mutually beneficial relationships with people who you can help and who can in turn help you. Most of the information you'll get is not from reading the newspaper or keeping up with the official releases from the campus administration. You'll get it from your peers. That's where the most current and relevant information is.

Suggested Networking Strategies

- **Get out and walk around**: Walking around the campus has many benefits aside from feeling refreshed. You'll run into an old acquaintance you wouldn't have taken the time to talk to otherwise or happen upon an administrator you've been dying to set up a meeting with.

- **Be a socialite**: Go to different types of events that will expose you to students on campus who care about very different activities than you do. It's important to know what all students are feeling and what they care about, not just the ones you hang out with or who share your values.

- **Go to other club meetings**: Most clubs never shy away from new people at their meetings. Make friends and interact with other club members, They are heavily involved in the campus and may have an interesting insight or two.

- **Share what interests you**: One thing that connects people the best is talking about their mutual passions. Share yours and find out what drives other students. You'll be well on your way to building your network and staying connected to the pulse of the campus.

- **Listen to everyone**: Each person comes from a different background which gives them a unique perspective on a current issue. Be careful not to exclusively listen to your friends or your work group because it may give you a narrow vision of the world.

Power Mapping and Elite Allies

Elite Allies are important to secure because they can bring many people to the table that would not otherwise come or be able to make high level decisions themselves. These are people who have influence, and you want to partner with them. Help them participate in an important action and have that action succeed through their participation. Having Elite Allies is especially important if you're trying to affect some change in campus policies or need an administrator to help make a connection with a community leader.

Power Mapping

1. Identify the important people you need to influence based on your plan.
2. Create a chart showing their relationships with each other. Include any friends or associates of these people that you know about.
3. Figure out who the lowest level person on the chart is that could get you what you want.
4. Work with this person to rectify your issue, and allow sufficient time for them to bring the problem to their superiors as needed.
5. Work with whatever person is handling the issue as it moves around within a particular department or as the issue rises through the ranks. Follow the lead of the people you're working with.
6. When you run into a problem, use your chart again to identify people who may be able to favorably influence the person who needs to make a decision.
7. Use your chart to keep track of who you've spoken to about which topics so you don't get confused.

Respecting Ranks

Always start with the lowest person who can help you and work your way up from there. Frequently a decision lies much lower down the totem pole than you think, and that person often has more time to help you.

Don't idly jump levels or go straight to the top: You can burn a lot of bridges by going over people's heads unnecessarily. Put in your due diligence working on the appropriate level and if you have evidence of them disregarding your concerns then go to their boss.

Finding and Being a Mentor

Mentors are very knowledgeable individuals that will help teach you what they know from years of personal experience. A mentor can be anyone from an older and more experienced student to an adult with years of experience in your field on interest. Frequently your club can have a faculty advisor to help fill this role for you and other leaders in your club. This is a person you identify with and have a special connection with. Mentors have a lot of impact on helping you understand you own priorities and getting you connected into the right places.

Why Mentors are Important

- **Knowledge**: Mentors have been through many problems that you are just beginning to encounter. If you are able to ask the right questions you'll learn how to master skills more quickly than most people. Mentors can help by going over problems you are having or issues you are facing and give you suggestions of actions to pursue.

- **Connections**: Mentors are connected in a wide network of people they've met and worked with over the years. Be specific about what you are interested in or want to pursue and they will have suggestion of people to talk to.

- **Support**: When you don't need anything except some motivation, a mentor can be invaluable in offering comments to get you back on track. Because they have been through a wide range of problems before, they are well equipped to give you positive feedback.

Become a Mentor

Just as important as finding a mentor to help you through your most difficult problems and motivational challenges, you can provide the same service to other students in your organization. Its important to share your unique knowledge with other students and foster leadership within your club. By passing along your experience you help build a stronger organization, equipped to deal with more complex problems in the future.

Summary

This chapter focuses on building a network of administrators, student leaders and student government members with the purpose of benefiting each other and the common goals. Coalition building brings groups of like-minded organizations with a variety of skills and focuses together in order to accomplish a goal. Keeping connected to other students and faculty at your school will also add to your project by giving you an insight into different aspects of the campus and conduits to people you need on your side. Helping others is just as important to creating a balanced relationship as receiving help yourself.

Chapter 6: Mobilize the Student Body

Some projects will require you to run a person to person campaign to influence students and mobilize them to take action whether its to get them out to our event or getting them to sign petitions for an issue you support. You can use a combination of methods to accomplish your goals: speak to students in person on the main stretch of campus at a table, go to their classroom to make a short announcement, and follow up with them through calls and online methods.

The Discounting Rule

You need to know how to estimate how many people you will need to contact to successfully reach your goals. This is a core component of planning for the success of your project. Below is a set of formulas you can use to help you estimate what you'll need to do to accomplish your goals for both mobilization and recruitment. Work backwards from your eventual objective to identify the intermediate targets you need to get there. For example, if you want to recruit 20 new volunteers for a voter registration drive, you need 40 students to say yes to do it. To get those 40 people you'll need to at least talk to 80 people. This means you'll need to get 160 people's contact information through one of the following methods.

Tabling for Petitions or Pledges

$$\frac{[\text{Confirmed Signatures}]}{15 \text{ per hour}} = [\text{Person-hours}] \qquad \frac{[\text{Person-hours}]}{[\text{Total Available Hours}]} = [\text{People per hour}]$$

Class Presentations

$$\frac{[\text{Contact Goal}]}{.15 \text{ (percent of the class)}} = [\text{Students to speak to}] \qquad \frac{[\text{Students to speak to}]}{[\text{Average class size}]} = [\text{Number of Classes}]$$

E-mail Lists

$$[\text{Contact Goal}] \ \mathsf{X} \ 400 \text{ E-mails per view} = [\text{People to E-mail}]$$

On-line Common Interest Groups

$$[\text{Contact Goal}] \ \mathsf{X} \ 40 \text{ Members per response} = [\text{People needed in the group}]$$

[ ] Denotes a number you put in or get out of the equation

Recruitment

One of the most frequent times your club will need to use these tips is recruiting new members at the beginning of the year. Recruitment can be an exciting time and an opportunity to really engage new people in your club and get them involved in a program you are putting on. These tried and true recruitment strategies will benefit you every time.

Planning your Recruitment

1. **Identify your needs**: Use the outline you made when you started planning your project. Does your club or event need 10 people or 100 people?

2. **Do the math**: Figure out how many contacts you need to make based on the formulas in this chapter.

3. **Figure out your strategies**: Identify what blend of methods to use to get to your target. Frequently one method will be more effective than another depending on who you're trying to reach.

4. **Schedule it in**: Build your recruitment plan with a set timeline and factor in when you want to achieve each set of targets.

5. **Get to it**: Share your recruitment plan with your team, get feedback, and make adjustments before beginning.

Contact Calling

[Recruitment Goal] **X** 2 **=** [Confirmed Yeses]

[Confirmed Yeses] **X** 2 **=** [Spoken with]

[Spoken with] **X** 2 **=** [Number of contacts needed]

Recruitment Tabling for Contact Info

$$\frac{[Contact\ info]}{5\ per\ hour} = [Person\text{-}hours]$$

$$\frac{[Person\text{-}hours]}{[Total\ Available\ Hours]} = [People\ per\ hour]$$

Class Presentations

$$\frac{[Contact\ info]}{.10\ (percent\ of\ the\ class)} = [Students\ to\ speak\ to]$$

$$\frac{[Students\ to\ speak\ to]}{[Average\ class\ size]} = [Number\ of\ Classes]$$

[ ] Denotes a number you put in or get out of the equation

Places to Recruit

- **High walking traffic areas**: Identify the main stretch of campus or a certain walking path that everyone goes through. You know your campus the best, so get out there and find those places

- **Large Classrooms**: Classes with 200-300 people can generate an average of 25 contact cards each for a few minutes of speaking so they are great places to recruit quickly and with little effort.

- **Student Union**: People around the student center are less hurried, more relaxed and more invested in the campus.

- **Outside the Library**: People going in and out of the library are there to study for extended periods of time, so talking to them is typically a welcome change of pace.

Start small, grow big: Once you start your recruitment drive get your new volunteers involved immediately by plugging them into the on-going recruitment effort. If you're short on enthusiastic people to do class presentations and have an amazing new volunteer, get him/her up to speed and out doing them! Constantly challenge and engage new people they'll be excited about doing more.

When to Recruit: Recruit when your fellow students are the least pre-occupied and have more time available. The hours around lunch are great because there are a lot of people on campus and they have at least a few moments to talk to you. The first few weeks of each quarter or semester work well. After most midterms are over and before the rush to study for finals works also.

Pre-Med Club
Interest Card

Name: _____

Phone: _____

E-Mail: _____

Interested in Volunteering? ☐

Pre-Med Club at Louisiana State University
http://www.lsu.edu/premedclub

Tabling

Tabling is the tried and true method for mobilizing your fellow students. Put a table out in a highly trafficked area of campus with a poster on display communicating the message about your cause. This involves active face to face contact with other students, engaging them in a short discussion about your club and getting them to take action in some form or another while they are walking by. You could be getting them to volunteer for a hunger awareness event, register to vote or sign a petition to make textbooks cheaper.

Tips for Tabling:

- **Be ACTIVE**: Nothing gets someone's attention like a stranger coming up and talking to them. It makes them feel important. Sitting behind a table may get you a couple interested people each hour, but engaging people face to face generates anywhere from 8-20 actions every hour, *per person*. Cut down the time you need to table by going out for a couple hours with a bunch of people and actively pursuing your goal.

- **The Smile and Wave**: When approaching people to talk to start about 10 feet away from the person. Make eye contact, smile and give them a small wave to get their attention.

- **Be friendly**: Present a calm and collected appearance. You might be nervous, but don't show it. You want to make people comfortable when talking to you.

- **Ask everyone**: Don't exclude people because they don't fit the "type" you're looking for – you'd be surprised just how many people will be supportive of your cause.

- **Practice**: If you're new to tabling or working on a new project, it always helps to run through the script with another person and pretend you are really doing it. This helps you identify your weak spots and build confidence in your abilities before being exposed to the real thing.

- **Shrug off rejection**: You'll talk to a lot of people who will not agree with you, give you the cold shoulder, or just plain ignore you. Don't let it get you down, because just around the corner you're going to find someone who really appreciates what you're doing.

- **Keep going**: Haven't managed to get any signatures on the petition despite being out asking people for an hour? It happens. Take a moment to review what you've been doing, practice with a friend, hone your skills and get back out there.

- **Develop your own style**: Once you become comfortable with the topic adjust the script to fit your personality. This makes your speech more genuine and will make you less nervous.

- **Remember to say thank you**: No matter what, always say thank you when parting from someone. They may have just ignored you, but at least they'll remember that you kept your cool and maybe they'll listen next time.

Sample Tabling Script: Text-books Affordability

[Make eye contact, smile, and wave from 10 feet away.]

—Hi! How are you today? Do you have a minute to sign this petition urging textbooks publishers to create unbundled versions of their textbooks?

—I'm part of the Student Advocacy Organization and we're working on making textbooks more affordable for students. Currently textbooks are bundled with materials that the majority of professors say has little to no value to their class. So last year, in conjunction with our faculty, we were able to set a policy of developing the basic teaching materials and books internally in the physics department. This year we're trying to achieve the same thing with the biology and statistics books.

—All we need is to demonstrate student's desire to have these books made by our faculty as an alternative to buying high priced books from the major publishers. [Hold out clipboard and petition] Will you sign this petition? It'll only take a minute.

—Would you be interested in helping out with this campaign?

—Thank you and have a great day!

Template Tabling Script:

The Catch: Make eye contact, smile and wave from about 10 feet away.

Intro: Greet them in a comfortable way. Be confident but not too forward. Ask them for exactly what you want. If they're not at all interested they'll let you know right away.

Problem: Say who you are and what you're working on. Explain why it is important that the person you are talking to take action immediately.

Solution: Present the actions you are taking to solve the problem and why they'll work.

Explain how they can help: Reassert your request for them to take action and how little work it will be on their part.

Finish: If they seem to be interested, ask if they want to help out and give them the opportunity. Thank them for their help and wish them well.

Class Presentations

Talking in front of hundreds of your peers can be a scary and exhilarating experience. Class presentations can be the most efficient use of your time because you can reach a large group of people in a matter of minutes. The downside is that it's large, impersonal, people can easily avoid listening to you and most people hate public speaking.

Tips for Class Presentations

- **Confidence is Key**: To mobilize a classroom full of students speak with authority. If you don't you risk of being ignored.

- **Practice**: Know the script, but more importantly know the material. You might accidentally skip or forget parts but the audience won't know you missed something as long as you don't stumble.

- **Talk Loudly**: Make sure you can be heard in the and that you can get the attention of people whispering to each other.

- **Move around**: Make simple hand motions, walk around, make eye contact with the audience. Be active to keep their attention.

- **Watch your posture**: Stand up straight and keep your body under control. Watch out for slouching, crossed legs, or hands behind your back, and avoid fidgeting. You want to look calm and confident.

- **Interact with the students**: Ask questions and force your audience to interact maybe by a show of hands. This gets them engaged in what you have to say.

- **Keep it short**: Your speech should be 2-3 minutes and not more than 5 minutes. Students' attention span is short, so get to the point asap.

Getting Clearance

Call and e-mail the professors for the classes you want to target prior to showing up at the beginning of the class. They will appreciate you asking permission and you can find out when is best to come. Frequently they'll tell you that one class day is better than another because of tests, important lectures, etc. Plan accordingly.

Sample Class Presentation Script: Voter Registration Drive

INTRODUCTION: Hi everyone, my name is _____ with the Voter Registration Initiative in the Student Advocacy Organization. I'd like to start off by thanking Professor _____ for allowing me to speak.

PROBLEM: How many of you are registered to vote? How many of you voted in the last election? Young people ages 18-24 vote at nearly half the rate that older people do. That means that politicians don't need our votes to get elected so they don't pay attention to issues that concern young people, like the high cost of higher education, affordable textbooks prices and a future we can look forward to.

SOLUTION: Over the next month we're registering students to vote all over the school and holding events to educate all of you about the major issues of this upcoming election. Our goal is to register over 2,000 new students to vote and turn out at least a quarter of the school to the polls on Election Day!

HOW THEY CAN HELP: If you have never registered to vote, we're passing around voter registration cards which we'll collect in a few minutes when you're done. If you've recently changed addresses you should register again at your current address. Remember to fill out the form completely and accurately otherwise you won't be registered to vote. We'll keep the information private, and we'll be dropping off the forms in the next few days.

WRAP-UP: When you're done please pass the forms to the center aisle and I will collect them in the next couple minutes. Thank you again for your attention and thank you professor _____. Have a great day!

Template Class Presentation Script:

Introduction: Who you are, what organization you're from. Remember to thank the professor!

Problem: Use your project's message to highlight important facts, statistics and stories about why it is important.

Solution: Present the actions you are taking to solve the problem and why they'll work.

How they can help: Be direct and tell the audience what they need to do to help, whether it is filling out a voter registration form or writing their contact info down.

Wrap-Up: Explain how you are going to collect the materials (give explicit instructions). Thank the audience and the professor again. Collect your things and go.

Contact Calling

This tool is one of the best methods for making sure things are going to happen. Getting confirmations for attendance, reminding someone that they signed up for an activity, or calling someone for the first time to get them involved can all be done very quickly and easily over the phone.

Tips for Contact Calling:

- **Be confident**: You'll frequently be calling someone while they are in the middle of doing something so be quick and polite. They did want you to call by filling out a contact form so don't feel like you're intruding.

- **Always confirm**: Many people will shy away from committing to a specific time, but be diligent in asking what time they can volunteer for or what meeting they are coming to. Don't count unconfirmed people in any totals because you can't guarantee that they'll show up since they didn't set a time.

- **Give alternatives**: Many people want to get involved but will not be able to make it to your primary activity, so give them alternative events where they can get connected.

- **Avoid leaving messages**: Do a second round of calling on a different day to try to talk to them on the phone. People will not usually return you call. Leaving a message closes the avenues to contact. You don't want to seem too aggressive by calling them again when they haven't even returned the first message.

- **Be prepared for callbacks**: Some people will call back later or the next day. Be prepared to explain what you were calling about and be able to answer questions without the script in front of you.

Sample Calling Script: Beginning of the Year Club Recruitment

Hi, can I speak with _____?

Hello, this is _____ with the Philosophy Club. How are you?

Good. I am calling because you filled out a contact card saying you were interested in getting involved in our organization. I just wanted to let you know that we're having an information session on Tuesday, September 30th at 7pm in room 125 in West Hall. Do you think you can make this?

[If yes, then mark off on attendance sheet.]

We're also having a tabling event outside of Strong Hall from 11am to 2pm the following day to get people signed up for our annual Battle of the Isms where we have people representing different philosophical backgrounds battling it out with their ideas. We'll be training people to help on the spot so don't worry if you haven't done this before. Can you help with this?

[If yes or maybe continue, otherwise skip to the end]

Which hour could you make it? We really want to make sure we have people committed to every time slot so we know what to expect.

Great! Thank you so much. We'll see you at _____ (date, time confirmed and location). Bye!

Online Organizing

Online communication and social networking websites provide a nearly endless array of possibilities for mobilizing your peers. They also come with drawbacks because of the sheer amount of content available. Don't solely use on-line strategies to achieve your goals. Make use of these methods as part of an overall plan incorporating both on-line and off-line mechanisms.

E-Mail:

- **Positives**: E-mail provides a quick and easy way to get information to fellow students. It generates a limited amount of action but requires very little time on your part.

- **Negatives**: Your e-mail will get deleted or ignored because of its inability to motivate action. You also have to compete with all the other e-mails being sent out.

- **How to use it to your advantage**: E-mail is mainly used to inform your target group. Keep it short and focused on the few priority events or issues. You can always give them a link to more information and actions they could take on a website if they're really interested.

Warning: On-line mechanisms are not substitutes to real, on the ground actions. They can be used to supplement the overall plan but not relied upon to generate success. On-line activities are too variable to count on them to help you succeed. They are too prone to overuse. Your audience will tune out.

Social Networking Sites:

- **Positives**: Groups, causes and event tools combined with widespread use among university students.

- **Negatives**: No guarantee that your efforts at mobilization will create action despite wide use by students.

- **How to use it to your advantage**

  a. Social networking sites are great for viral or word of mouth mobilization. Allow enough time for this to work. Use the groups to have your friends invite their friends and have their friends invite more friends for all sorts of common interest groups. You can then use this group to disseminate information or attempt to mobilize them for an event.

  b. When preparing for an event, create an event invitation far enough in advance so that a reasonable amount of people can see the event is taking place. This also helps to get a good minimum estimate of attendance.

  c. Groups can also help to bring together students around a central and clearly defined cause. There are also many functions like donations, announcements, and recruitment that make a good choice for mobilizing around issues.

Instant Messaging:

- **Positives**: You can disseminate information quickly through people's social networks, especially when it calls for immediate action, like reminding people to vote on Election Day.

- **Negatives**: You can never tell how far the message will penetrate or whether people will be willing to participate by passing it along.

- **How to use it to your advantage**: Make a very short message – one sentence or a link. Make it matter. Make sure this is a message you would be willing to send out to your buddy list.

Retention

You can't forget about all the people that make your organization or events so successful day after day. Most people who get involved in an organization genuinely care about success of the club. That doesn't mean that their passion is inexhaustible or that they'll stay around if they are treated poorly. This is why retaining your leaders and volunteers is so important. They represent the compilation of experience and knowledge that drives your successful projects day in and day out.

Suggestions for Retention:

- **Be real**: Nothing spoils the mood like fake appreciation. Be authentically invested in your club members and show interest in their lives.

- **Be honest**: If there are problems with the event or project try to figure out a way to incorporate everyone into fixing it. Make it a team effort rather than an individual call.

- **Build a relationship**: Get to know each other outside of the organization activities. Arrange for your team to grab something to eat after long work sessions or plan a club wide outing. Some of the best and most effective projects are done by people who love to work together and have fun together.

- **Make work fun**: People will do an amazing amount of work without any kind of reward except their own gratification, but if you can throw a little fun into a draining task it can boost motivation.

Summary

Mobilizing the student body is one of the most time and energy intensive activities your club can engage in. Person to person organizing relies on a great deal of planning and identifying important target numbers to reach in order to achieve success. One of the first parts of student mobilization is recruitment of students into the club so you'll have enough people to engage students on your campus. This is normally achieved through one of the primary mobilizing strategies. Once you've identified the needs for your project, there are number of strategies to use to achieve your goal: getting a table out on the main stretch of campus, speaking to large classrooms before class starts, calling people interested or committed to the cause, and mobilizing students on-line. The right combination of strategies will help you achieve success with your project, and allow both you and your group to be rewarded for their achievement.

Chapter 7: Planning - The Key to Winning

Planning is an outline of your programs, starting with establishing your goals and going through every step you need to take to accomplish those goals. To win you have to be willing to achieve all the incremental steps along the way. If you try to do all aspects of the project without planning, your lofty ideas will fall flat on their face. Planning is the most important part of initiating any new activity. It makes every part of the project come together in an organized and orderly way.

Planning takes into account nearly every skill and concept covered in this manual. If you haven't spent a few minutes reviewing the general concepts do that now so you know what to put in the plan. Take the time on the front end of your project to put together a good, well thought out plan. This will save you from a lot of stress and wasted effort later in the project.

Beware: All too often people will wait until the last minute and try to get everything done at once. Avoid the stress and the frantic last minute mess by putting in the work on the front end to figure out what things need to get done and when. This ensures you don't forget something important.

Saving Your Precious Time by Spending Time Planning

The more prepared and organized you are the more time you'll save by not wasting it on the activities you'd rather not be doing. It seems counterintuitive that the extra task of planning out your week, month, or semester would give you more time. It will keep you on track for your goals and avoid the unimportant and ineffective tasks.

Work Backwards

Once you've determined when you want to achieve victory or hold your event its time to think about how and when you need to execute each of your strategies. Start from the day of the event or campaign victory and think back through each day and week leading up to the event. Determine what things need to happen and in which order so that will result in achieving your goal or reaching the next step of your plan. There is no quick way to do this step because you must think back through every step you will need to take. This involves working through one strategy all the way to the beginning and may require you to utilize multiple different strategies in order to achieve your final targets.

For example, let's say your publicity target is to hang 400 posters the week before an event. After thinking about the actual mechanics of putting up the posters, you determine that to get them put up you need to have the posters printed and a team of people confirmed to put them up on a specific day. You'll need to do those things the week before. To get to the week 3 actions you'll need to have the poster design sent out to get printed, but you'll also need to recruit people this week so you'll have everything set the following week. Finally, the week before this you need to design the poster and get it approved.

Working backwards helps you make sure you plan for all the details that each task will require by evaluating what you need to do to get to each successive step. Make sure you accomplish all the tasks early enough to be able to stick to the timeline and accomplish your goal on time.

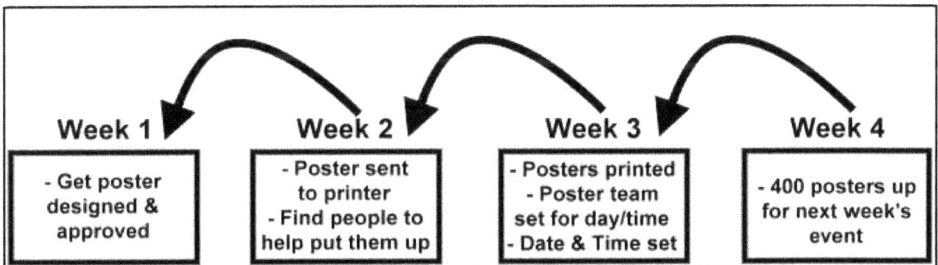

Week 1	Week 2	Week 3	Week 4
- Get poster designed & approved	- Poster sent to printer - Find people to help put them up	- Posters printed - Poster team set for day/time - Date & Time set	- 400 posters up for next week's event

Make a Weekly Action Plan

Doing weekly plans is one of the underappreciated gems of planning that allows you to spend your time wisely. Get a planner to help you keep on top of the tasks you decide you need to do each day. Get into the habit of doing this and you will have more free time and a lot less stress. Take your plans for this week from your long term plan and figure out what you need to do each day and how much time you think it will take. (See Template Weekly Action Plan in this chapter)

- **Pick out your primary priorities for the week**: Keep a list of priorities around two or three. Keep your attention focused on completing the most important tasks rather than getting bogged down in unimportant and ineffective tasks (See Setting Priorities & Time Management)

- **Fill in the target objectives you want to accomplish**: This could be your recruitment goals for your upcoming event, people you need to meet with or even a big essay you need to devote time to working on. By writing down the details and numerical goals you'll be able to measure your progress towards getting everything done.

Stressed and Don't have Enough Time to do a Weekly Plan? Think Again!

How much time to do spend every week on time wasting activities? Probably more than the hour it takes to plan your week, doing something you don't want or have to do. Instead, put that time to good use by planning out the week ahead and you'll find you have even more time to do what you really want to do.

Note: To make the best use of your weekly plan consider including other responsibilities like homework or other clubs you are involved in so you have a truly accurate and personalized schedule.

- **Break targets down by day**: Write down each activity that needs to get done and how much time you think it would take next to each day of the week. Set specific time limits on all tasks in your planner. (See Time Management for methods on scheduling your time)

- **Set daily priorities**: Figure out what tasks absolutely need to get done each day. These should be the first tasks you work on each day because there will be distractions that come up throughout the day that will take away from your available time.

- **Leave space for free time:** This will prevent you from over-working yourself to the point of exhaustion. Just because you can save time by doing things more effectively it doesn't mean you should fill it with more work. Leaving some time will give you some leeway when new things come up or projects take longer.

- **Put a limit on the work you do:** More work is not necessarily better work. Give yourself a chance to do a really good job on a couple of activities rather than spreading yourself across too many.

Weekly Action Plan

Name: Alexis Madison
Position: VP of Recruitment
Week: January   21st — 27th

Major Priorities:
1.) Meet with the Dean of Students
2.) Write   winter recruitment plan
3.) Train new intern

Priorities	Objectives and Targets	Check-Off
Priority #1: Meet with the Dean of Students	Meet with the Dean to brainstorm ways to get more students involved in clubs	
Priority #2: Write winter recruit-ment plan	Complete writing a detailed plan and timeline to recruit new club members	
Priority #3: Train new volunteers	Prepare handout and brief leader-ship training for new volunteers	X
Schoolwork:	Read 40 pages for history for Tues-day, 6-8 page essay in sociology due Thursday	X
Other Responsi-bilities:	Attend Student Council meeting to discuss a new event that is coming up	
People to meet with:	Meet with new volunteers to deter-mine their areas of interest and get them involved	X
Prep Work for Next Week:	E-mail club leaders to get ideas to present about the recruitment plan.	

Day by Day Outline:
Monday: Write Vol. Summary (11am-12pm)
Read for history (1-2pm, 8-10pm)
Tuesday: Training handout (2-3pm)
Student Council meeting (5-6pm)
Work on essay (6-9pm)
Wednesday: Prep for Dean meeting (3-4pm)
Prep for club meeting (4-5pm)
Work on essay (8-11pm)
Thursday: Meeting with Dean of Stu-dents (12-1pm)
Club Meeting (7-8:30pm)

Friday: Volunteers meeting (9-10am)
E-mail club leaders for recruitment ideas (10-10:30am)
Saturday: E-mail new club members (1-1:30pm)
Sunday: Write Winter Recruitment Plan (2-4pm)

Total Club Hours: 10.5 hours

Steps to Effective Planning

Planning is a long and involved process to outline your path to success. Throughout these steps we'll use an example to help you absorb the concepts at each step. Let's start with the example that you want to put on a major fundraising event to support your favorite charity and you're thinking about some kind of dance expo.

- **Brainstorming**: Before you start putting down any specifics goals and objectives take some time to mull over the problem you want to address. Get excited – think about different aspects of the problem, and creative ways to solve it.

- **Find your Vision**: The overall objective you want to achieve. Make it as broad as necessary to encompass your vision.

- **Establish your Goals**: Using your vision, determine a specific objective you want to accomplish. What would you consider an accomplishment or a victory?

Dance-Off Fundraiser Project Planning:

-- Brainstorming: Our club wants to raise money to donate to an after school children's program. A competition could bring in a lot of different groups as well as their friends.

-- Vision: We want to put on amazing events for a large portion of the student body to have fun at and contribute to a good cause.

-- Goals: Put on a dance competition fundraising event that pits different dancers and/or dance groups against each other. We want to raise $5,000 for our charity and $5,000 for the charity of choice for the winning dance group and have at least 1,000 people in attendance.

- **Select Appropriate Strategies**: Strategies are methods you use to achieve your goal such as using "visibility" for putting up posters or "recruitment" when you need to get more people involved. The specifics of these strategies are in Chapter 6. Skim them to know what you have at your disposal.

-- Strategies

Visibility: Posters, Fliers, Online

Recruitment: Tabling, Class presentations, Calling

Media: Campus paper articles, campus radio

Mobilization: Tabling, Calling

Coalition Building: Campus Administration, Faculty, Clubs and Organizations

- **Set your Targets**: Targets should be a specific number you are shooting for that will be sufficient to achieve your goals. Your targets should *never* be arbitrary, but represent an educated guess at what you think you need to achieve success. More is not always better. Keep what you consider a victory in mind and what you honestly think it will take to get you there. In this section you will calculate the intermediate goals you need to hit in order to achieve your objectives using the discounting rule. (See Student Mobilization)

-- Targets

Goal Target: Your goal is to get about **1,000 students to attend** the event. Based on the discounting rule you need to get confirmations on attendance for twice that amount, which is **2,000**. On the days before the event we need to be confident that we are going to reach our target numbers, so we will use more of the discounting rule to figure out how to get there.

Attendance: Since each of the strategies depend on how we reach the attendance goal, we decide we are going to get half of the direct commitments (and phone numbers so we can confirm later) from tabling and use other methods to mobilize the rest. The **1000 from tabling** can be calculated using the following: your team can get about **15 confirmed contacts per hour**, so that is **67 person-hours** of tabling which, if we plan on tabling for 2 hours each day, the two weeks leading up to the event (2 hr/day x 5 days/week x 2 weeks = 20 hrs), we need about **3-4 people every hour (67 person-hours / 20 total hours = 3.35 people per hour)**.

Because people occasionally cannot make it we will schedule **134 person-hours**, twice as many as we need. We decide that each person who is on the team will be really committed and will agree to do an average of 10 hours over the two weeks leading up to the event. This means that we need to **recruit 14 people** for the team for tabling (134 person-hrs/10 hrs per person = 14 people). We decide we can get about half of those people (7 club members) from within the club, and **recruit 7 more** during the initial week of tabling.

This part of the example only covered one of the strategies from step #4 and you can already see how complicated but important this planning step is. Take a look at the sample plan for a more detailed diagram of the entire campaign.

- **Create a Timetable**: Figure out when you want to accomplish your goal and successfully execute each of your strategies. Set it at a reasonable and appropriate time in the future. Concerts can rarely be put together in a week, and a media generating event works best when it coincides with the major event you are trying to affect. One strategy will need to be completed before another can commence. To determine how and when to reach each of your targets use the backwards planning model which we've already practiced while doing targeting estimates.

-- **Timetable:** We need to have at least 7 club members ready to go two weeks before the event for tabling alone. To get there we need to have everyone trained the week before. To get people to the training we need to have a date, time, and location set the week before that. We also need to have our team members set the week before the training so we can get them there, which means the week prior if not two weeks before we need to send out an announcement to the entire club to get people to volunteer, as well as asking around and recruiting people.

	GOALS	WEEK 1	WEEK 2	WEEK 3	WEEK 4	WEEK 5	WEEK 6	WEEK 7	DAY OF
VISIBILITY	~ 100 Posters up 2 weeks before; ~1 campus -wide e-mail each of two weeks leading up to event			~Design posters; ~Brainstorm and develop message	~Make posters and advertising materials	~Submit request for campus wide e-mail for next two weeks; ~More poster and material making	~Put up 50 posters; ~E-mail message	~Put up 50 posters; ~E-mail message	
VOLUNTEERS	~ 14 Students for tabling; ~ 10 Student for class presentations			~Recruit volunteers from our club (7-10); ~Recruit from other clubs (5)	~Volunteers help make materials	~Volunteer training for tabling & class presentations; ~Volunteers help create materials for event	~Recruit volunteers from tabling/class presentations (5-8)	~Day-of logistics training	~All volunteers at event, helping run the program
ACTIVE EVENTS	~ 1 table out for 2 hours each day 2 weeks leading up to the event (100 conf. attendees/day); ~ Class annoucements to boost attendance (80 conf. attendees/day)				~Create contact list of Professors	~Reserve space for table; ~Contact professors for class presentations	~Table outside Student Center to sell tickets/invites; ~Class announcements to get invites	~Table outside Student Center to sell tickets/invites; ~Class announcements to get invites	~Sell tickets outside the venue
COALITION BUILDING	~ Club leaders take active part in planning and executing the event	~Contact club leaders to attend brainstorming meeting the following week	~Planning meeting		~Go to club meetings to recruit volunteers		~Get club leaders involved in planning day-of logistics	~Day-of logistics review with leaders	
ONLINE	~Invite 4,000 to online event				~Event group created	~400 invited, 100 accepted	~1200 invited, 300 accepted	~2400 invited, 600 accepted	~1,000 people RSVPed to event
LOGISTICS	~ 1,000 Students at Prom	~Research campus dance teams; ~Contact prospective teams	~Brainstorm themes and decorations; ~Reserve location for event	~Start signing dance teams	~Purchase decoration materials; ~Review logistics for event and the plan to get everything done	~Begin putting together decorations	~Finalize decrations and materials; ~Final dance groups and	~Ticket sales end (Friday)	~Go early and put up decorations with volunteers; ~1,000 Students at event (Friday Night)

Planning Events

Putting on large and small scale events is one of the most common activities that student clubs can do. Planning for these events follows the same practices as any other type of project, with a couple of special notes. As part of your planning for the quarter/semester or year you should always include the events you plan on doing. This section will provide a few tips for specifically planning events.

- **Think Ahead**: Starting the planning process early will add to a great event idea. Many events suffer from a lack of planning, and especially planning early enough to get everything done. Don't put off planning and throw something together at the last minute.

- **Details, Details, Details**: Events often require many more details to be completed to make it amazing. This is why procrastination and poor preparation are the blight of event planning. Be sure to write down everything you need to get done, down to every detail. This practice will pay off in the long run with less stress and a better event.

> *Minimum* **Recommended Event Planning start time**:
>
> Petition/Tabling: 2 weeks
>
> Social/Fun: 2-3 weeks
>
> Press/Media: 3 weeks
>
> Entertainment: 1-2 months
>
> Action/Protest: 2-3 months
>
> Fundraisers: 2-3 months
>
> Major Concerts: 4-6 months

- **Fun and exciting events vs. effective but boring**: All work and no play may get you to your goals this time, but that may be as far as you get. As much as we like to think of ourselves and others as work machines it just isn't the case. Just because something may seem less effective, doesn't mean you won't get a boost from an intangible result known as fun and excitement. An example could be building a costume themed after your issue for the campus Halloween festival. This generates a buzz around the issue but also lets the group have fun by running around the festival. Throw in some fun events with the rest of your schedule. Find a balance between fun and practical activities that still lets you achieve the goals you set out to accomplish.

How to Use Your Plan

- **Re-evaluate your plan at least once a week:** Figure out if you've kept up with the goals and timeline. If not, try to determine why you're off track.

- **Adjust your plan as needed:** If you're off track figure out what you have to do to still hit your goals. If necessary, adjust your goal up or down if it's no longer realistic. Add new projects and events that come up during the quarter. Don't feel boxed in to the original plan. Take advantage of new opportunities that present themselves.

- **Choose your weekly priorities based on your plan:** What are the most important things to focus on this week? Today? Pick things that absolutely have to get done. Stay on track by having a clear vision of what needs to be done.

- **Use your plan to figure out what you realistically can expect to get done:** Everything that you cannot get done yourself delegate to others. Use the plan to delegate tasks and help ensure that more is going on than only what you have time to do.

Avoiding Planning Pitfalls

- **Don't dishearten if your plan isn't working**: Don't stop using your plan if doesn't work exactly as you had planned. Plans look very different by the time you are done. Things are always changing. Take time to re-evaluate the original plan and strategize new solutions. You may be on the right track, but just need a few tweaks.

- **Plans only work if you follow them**: If you write the plan and then don't look at it again it is useless. Once you've put all the work into your plan follow through on your goals.

- **Avoiding planning will put off your goals**: Sometimes things work out without any planning at all. Most of the time it will not work that way, or at least not the way you want. If you want to achieve your goals: plan, plan early, and plan often.

- **Stay away from overall goals that are vague or un-achievable**: You want to know what you're working towards and know when you've succeeded. Shooting for a realistically ambitious goal is much more likely to succeed than setting your weight against gigantic problems. World peace is a great goal but its going to require a much, much longer plan.

- **Mind your surroundings and do your research**: Know the status and situation of your issue. Know who else is passionate about it and who opposes it. The more you know the better you'll be able to custom tailor your plan to achieve victory. Make the plan fit reality and you'll achieve it!

Summary:

Planning your project relies on skills covered in every chapter of this manual and integrates all the strategies you decide you need to use. Planning before you start your project will save you far more time and energy during execution. Working backwards allows you to identify the intermediate targets you need to hit in order to hit your overall targets later. The steps to planning allow you to build the scale and objectives of your project in a methodical way so that all of your goals come from realistic targets. You can also use the Weekly Action Plan to break down your plan ever farther to identify your most important objectives to accomplish each week.

Glossary

Class Presentation: Giving a short 2-3 minute speech in a classroom full of students in order to mobilize them into action, informing them about some important news, and find the people interested in volunteering. This strategy is effective in generating contact information from pledges or interest in a certain issue which can be used to follow up when the date of an event or action is coming up.

Coalition Building: Forming an organization out of a number of separate groups interested in accomplishing the same goal. This allows different parts of the coalition to focus on their strengths and pool their resources for the benefit of the cause or project.

Contact Calling: Is a method for getting confirmations and identifying people interested in a particular campaign or project. Contact information is typically collected from tabling or class presentations. Calling ensures that individuals get connected into the project or reminded about an event.

Discounting Rule: When planning your project you use the discounting rule to estimate the numerical intermediate goals that you need to hit in order to reach your overall goal.

Goals: With regard to planning, your goals are the tangible results you want to have at the end of your project.

Messaging: Is the way of phrasing statements connected with your project in order to communicate with your target groups in the most effective way possible.

Parliamentary Procedure: The rules that guide official decision making in groups that have adopted these guidelines. They allow equal debate and decision making in a group.

Postering: This involves putting up posters and other advertising material up around your campus in order to publicize an event or project.

Power Mapping: A way of charting out the power structure of important decision makers and potential allies that have influence over achieving the goal of your project.

Press Advisory: This is an invitation for an event that is sent to members of the press to let them know what is going on and invite them to come and report on the activity.

Press Release: A complete article written as the ideal story that is reported. It is send to the press with all the information they need to write an article of their own.

Recruitment: A term for getting students involved in a project that needs additional help and more people to get the goals accomplished.

Retention: A method for keeping volunteers and leaders involved in the project or organization.

Strategy: A method or type of action used in accomplishing a goal for a project.

Table/Tabling: Tabling is a strategy for mobilizing the student body. Students will put out a table with informational materials and frequently an eye catching banner or visual to draw other students' attention. The main goal of the table is to generate action by actively approaching students in a friendly way while they walk by in order to ask them to help take action or inform them about an important issue that affects them.

Target: Specific numerical or tangible results that you need to accomplish using the strategies chosen for your project.

Vision: The aspirational objective you are trying to achieve with your project. This should be a general and inspiring statement of what you are trying to achieve.

Weekly Action Plan: A plan for your week, taking objectives from your long term plan and fitting them into your schedule so that you can accomplish them in an orderly way.

www.ingramcontent.com/pod-product-compliance
Lightning Source LLC
Chambersburg PA
CBHW072209270326
41930CB00011B/2595